TIME-TRAVEL GUIDES

The MAYA

BEN HUBBARD

Gareth Stevens PUBLISHING

Please visit our website, www.garethstevens.com. For a free color catalog of all our high-quality books, call toll free 1-800-542-2595 or fax 1-877-542-2596.

Cataloging-in-Publication Data

Names: Hubbard, Ben, 1973-, author.
Title: The Maya / Ben Hubbard.
Description: Buffalo, NY : Gareth Stevens Publishing, 2026. |
Series: Time-travel guides | Includes glossary and index.
Identifiers: ISBN 9781482475456 (pbk.) | ISBN 9781482475463 (library bound) |
ISBN 9781482475470 (ebook)
Subjects: LCSH: Mayas--Juvenile literature. | Mayas--Civilization--Juvenile literature. |
Mayas--History--Juvenile literature. | Mayas--Social life and customs--Juvenile literature.
Classification: LCC F1435.H78 2026 | DDC 972.81'016--dc23

Published in 2026 by
Gareth Stevens Publishing
2544 Clinton St.
Buffalo, NY 14224

First published in Great Britain in 2022 by Hodder & Stoughton

Artwork and Design: Collaborate Agency
Editor: Sarah Silver

Picture credits:
p.4-5: © johnbraid/Shutterstock.com, p.28: © Vincenzo Iacovoni/Shutterstock.com,

Printed in China
CPSIA compliance information: Batch #QW26GS: For further information contact Gareth Stevens at 1-800-542-2595.

CONTENTS

CHICHÉN ITZÁ

Welcome to Chichén Itzá – the dazzling Mayan city that became a very powerful place between 950 and 1200 CE. At its peak, Chichén Itzá was an awe-inspiring complex of pyramids, temples, ball courts, and roads that over 30,000 people called home. Later it was abandoned and was reclaimed by the jungle, only to be rediscovered centuries later.

TIME-TRAVEL GUIDES

Your time-travel guide

Congratulations for buying this Time-Travel Guidebook – the must-have companion for travelers journeying into the past. The guidebook will give you expert advice on where to stay, what to see, and how best to spend your time at Chichén Itzá. Top travel tips throughout will give you the low-down on what to bring, where to shop, and which local delicacies to sample.

Journey back

In the 21st century, archaeologists visit the site (shown here) to try and understand the people who lived at Chichén Itzá. But now, with time-travel technology, we can journey back to find out for ourselves. So buckle up and prepare to beam in to this magnificent and mysterious Mayan city.

Top Tip

Look out for

Jaguars, ocelots, pumas, and other big cats live in the jungle around Chichén Itzá. But don't be scared – Chichén Itzá nobles also wear the skins of these animals as clothes.

Top Tip

What to pack

Plasters. The people of Chichén Itzá believe they need to spill blood to please their gods. They do this by poking sharp points through parts of their bodies. If you are tempted to join in, maybe a small pin prick will be enough.

PUTTING CHICHÉN ITZÁ ON THE MAP

Construction of Chichén Itzá began in around 455 CE and it was built up by different rulers over several centuries. Today, Chichén Itzá is made up of a complex of stone buildings that cover 4 square miles (10 sq km) of Mexico's Yucatan Peninsula. This map has highlighted the key areas of interest in Chichén Itzá for time-traveling visitors. To learn more about each highlighted area, simply turn to the page numbers on the map key.

Where is Chichén Itzá?

There are many Mayan city-states in the region of Mesoamerica, which covers the 21st century countries of Mexico, Belize, Guatemala, Honduras, El Salvador, and Nicaragua. Many major Mayan cities have been constructed in the jungles of the Mesoamerican lowlands. Chichén Itzá, however, is located near the coast. This is good news for time travelers who love to swim in the sea.

A brief Mayan history

Early Mayan people were farmers who built their villages in around 1500 BCE. By 200 CE they were building large cities for thousands of people. However, by around 900 CE, most of the large cities were abandoned. Chichén Itzá became the main Mayan city and was ruled over by a group called the Itzá until around 1200. Chichén Itzá means "at the mouth of the well of the Itzá." Look out for the natural wells, called cenotes, as you travel around the city.

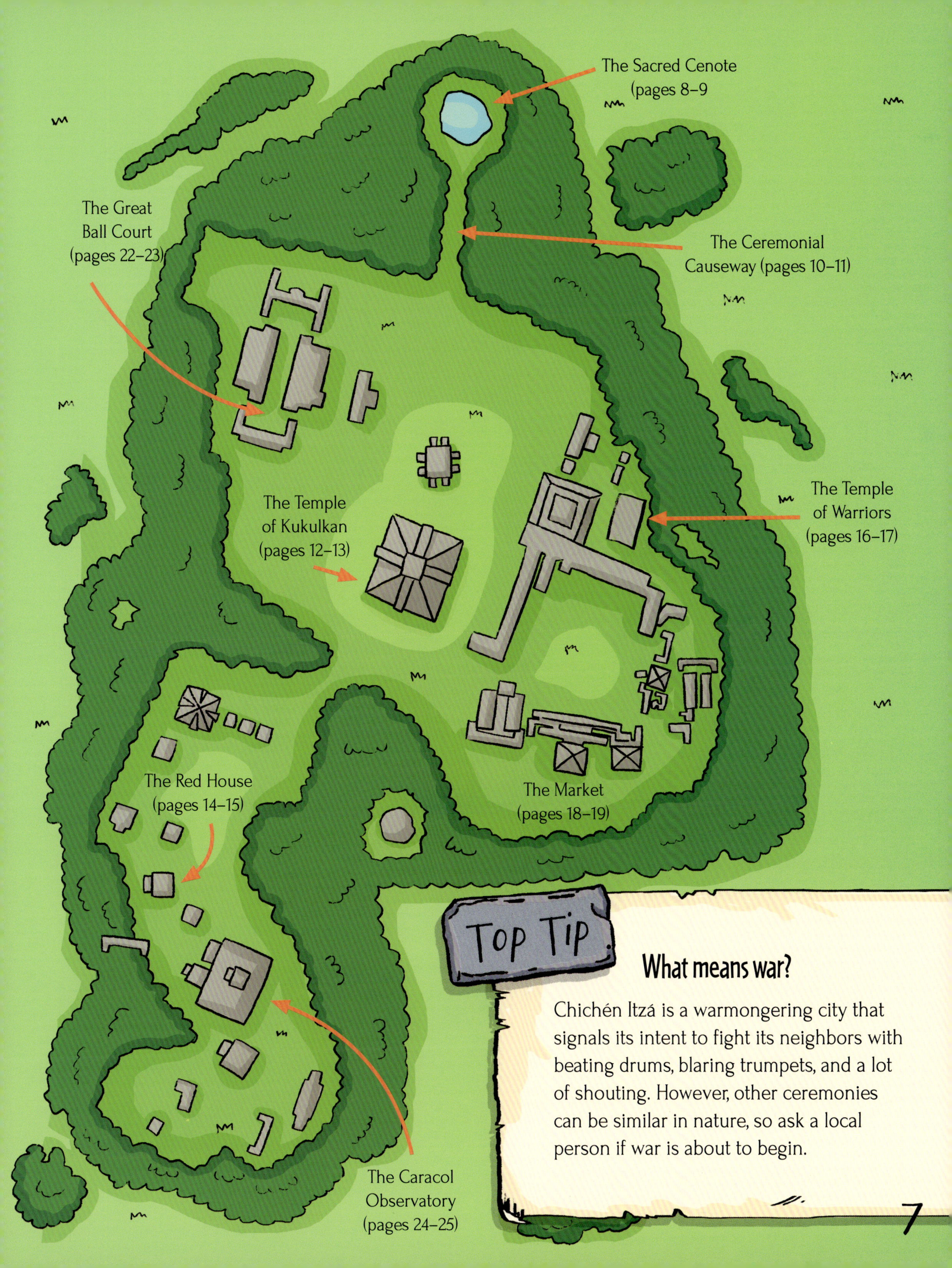

Top Tip

What means war?

Chichén Itzá is a warmongering city that signals its intent to fight its neighbors with beating drums, blaring trumpets, and a lot of shouting. However, other ceremonies can be similar in nature, so ask a local person if war is about to begin.

STARE INTO THE SACRIFICIAL WATER

Time travelers typically begin their Chichén Itzá stay at the Sacred Cenote – an underground well situated just outside the city. Chichén Itzá has several cenotes that provide people with vital fresh water. The people of Chichén Itzá make offerings and sacrifices into the Sacred Cenote so that their gods do not let the water run dry.

Sacred sacrifice

Time travelers worried about running out of water during their stay can make an offering at the Sacred Cenote. The people of Chichén Itzá often throw in their prized possessions, such as copper bells, jade figurines, and gold masks. However, they also sacrifice people, including children. The sacrificial victims are usually prisoners of war taken after battle.

Top Tip

Watch out for...

Monkeys. The Maya believe that before using maize, the gods made people out of clay and then wood. The wooden people had no respect for the gods so they were chased into the jungle. Here, it is believed, they became the monkeys you can see around Chichén Itzá today.

People of the maize

The Maya believe their gods made humans from maize (corn). Maize, the staple food, and water to grow it are therefore of great importance to the Maya. At the Sacred Cenote, offerings are made to the rain god Chaac, so he will provide water for the crops.

WALK INTO THE CITY

From the Sacred Cenote, time travelers can walk along the Ceremonial Causeway into the city. This is one of dozens of roads connecting Chichén Itzá and the surrounding region. These roads help the Chichén Itzá ruler to communicate with his people and allow trade to reach the city.

How to build a Mayan road

To time travelers from the future, Mayan roads may not look like anything special. They are, however, a marvel of ancient engineering. Built from layers of cut rock and rubble, the sides of the roads are made strong with large boulders and paved on top with bright white limestone. This ensures each road is solid and raised off the jungle floor around it.

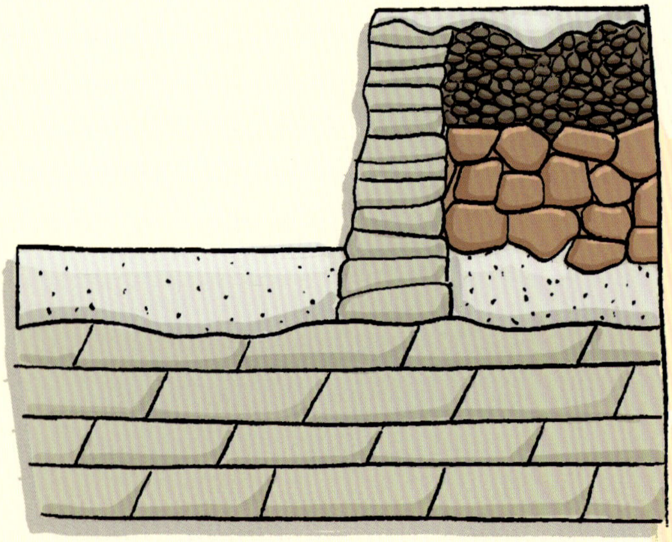

Spot the traveling traders

Visitors to Chichén Itzá should look out for merchants who carry a fan, a walking stick, and a bag to identify who they are. Among the many trade objects merchants bring in and out of Chichén Itzá are salt, quetzal feathers, jade stones, and stingray spines. Stingray spines are used to make a body part, such as the tongue, bleed. This is an offering to the gods.

Top Tip

Watch out for...

Praying road users. It is customary in Chichén Itzá to say a prayer to the gods when crossing a road. Make sure to leave them in peace as you pass by.

SEE THE SERPENT TEMPLE

Time travelers will be awed by the towering Temple of Kukulkan, which stands at the center of Chichén Itzá. Dedicated to the serpent god Kukulkan, the temple is where the city's priests communicate with the gods and perform ceremonies and rituals before a crowd.

Stay for the serpent ceremony

A must-see ceremony for visitors takes place during the spring and autumn equinoxes. This is when the last rays of the sun catch the serpent sculptures on the temple steps, making them look like they are crawling down to the bottom. As this takes place, priests burn incense from the top of the temple and there is chanting from the crowd below.

Top Tip

Count the steps

Every part of the Temple of Kukulkan has been built with symbolic meaning. The 91 steps on each side combined with the final step on the top equals 365 – the number of days in the year. Energetic visitors can climb each side to check!

Walk to the top

The priests have given permission for time travelers to climb to the top of the 78-foot (24 m) high Temple of Kukulkan. This is a steep climb, so take a moment to marvel at the construction. The temple has been built from thousands of limestone blocks, all cut to size using stone tools. More amazingly still, today's temple has been built over an older, smaller temple, which was originally built over a cenote!

Top Tip

Peek at the jaguar

Although usually closed to visitors, there is a door at the top of the temple leading into the original pyramid. This contains rare treasures: a Chacmool figure (see page 16) and a jaguar statue painted red with jade spots and white flint teeth. Ask a helpful priest if you can take a peek!

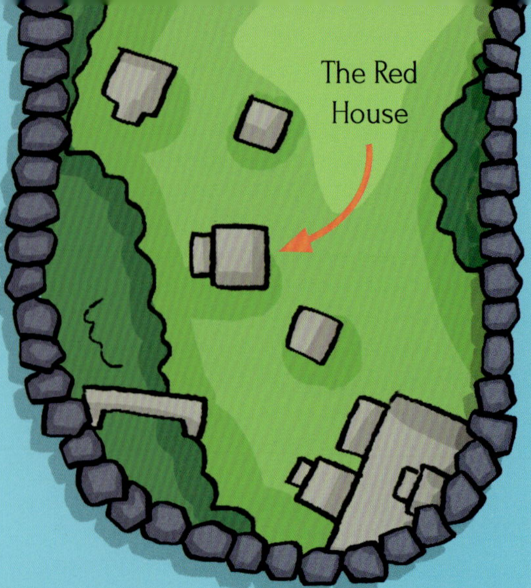

WHERE TO STAY

To experience luxury-living in Chichén Itzá, a stay at the Red House can be arranged. The Red House is a royal residence, raised on a high platform and richly decorated with ornate wall carvings and a lavish red interior. Only the most important people – and time travelers – have the privilege of visiting.

Food for feasting

The Mayan rulers, nobles, and priests hold grand parties with feasting, music, dancing, and storytelling. Time-traveling guests can attend such an event at the Red House. Here, servants will bring you avocado, papaya, chilli peppers, sweet potatoes, squash, and tomatoes. You'll also be fed the typical Mayan maize tortilla, a flat cake often filled with beans, vegetables, and chili paste. Meat-eating time travelers will be able to feast on deer, monkeys, iguanas, and the long-snouted tapir. A drink made from fermented maize and honey will also be served – but it's not for kids!

Top Tip

Don't choke on the cacao

Cacao beans are the most valuable foodstuff in the Mayan world and only enjoyed by the rich and powerful. The beans are made into a thick drinking chocolate that is spiced with chili and tastes very bitter. However, make sure not to choke on the drink as it will be a great insult to your hosts!

Stay in an everyday home

While the Chichén Itzá nobles live in large stone buildings, peasants and workers live in simple wooden homes with whitewashed walls and roofs thatched with jungle leaves. Inside, the houses have earth floors, pots for storing food, and hammocks to sleep in. It is cheap to stay in a peasant's hut and highly recommended as an authentic Mayan experience.

WATCH THE WARRIORS

The rulers of Chichén Itzá are protected by two things – a wealthy society and a powerful military. It is the job of Chichén Itzá's warriors to protect the elite and fight against neighboring cities. These wars provide a vital source of prisoners for human sacrifice. Time travelers can check out carvings of these gruesome rituals when they visit the Temple of Warriors.

Don't tremble at the temple

The Temple of Warriors is a scary sight. It features feathered serpent columns and carvings of warriors, eagles, and jaguars devouring human hearts. At the top is an altar and statue of Chacmool. Chacmool is a mysterious god shown lying down with a bowl on his stomach to receive offerings. Human sacrifice is performed at the temple, so those time travelers with weak stomachs should end their visit at the carvings below.

Top Tip

Watch out for...

Fat dogs. Many years ago, the Maya tamed wild dogs but they also sometimes fattened them up and ate them for food. Other dogs are sacrificed to the gods, while some are simply pets.

What do warriors wear?

Mayan warriors include members from all levels of society, from nobles to peasants. Visitors to Chichén Itzá can tell the warriors apart by their different outfits. Ordinary warriors paint their bodies black and red, carry wooden clubs, slingshots, and spears, and wear thick cotton breastplates. The top warriors are easy to spot – they wear jaguar skins and quetzal feathers.

TIME TO SHOP

After the unnerving Temple of Warriors, time travelers can unwind with a visit to the market. Stroll past the stalls selling local handicrafts as well as exotic, exported goods from around Mesoamerica. Market days are a special occasion in Chichén Itzá, where merchants come from all over and market judges make sure no one is being cheated.

Buy some handicrafts

Chichén Itzá is famous for its rubber objects and painted vases. The rubber is extracted in liquid form from rubber trees to make balls and small, human-like statues. These statues are often thrown into the Sacred Cenote as offerings. Visitors to the market will also find an abundance of Mayan textiles woven in bright colors and patterns.

Top Tip

Look out for ...

Masks made of hammered gold. Gold is rare in other Mayan cities, so these gold masks prove that Chichén Itzá's trade routes reach as far as modern Panama and Colombia, where the gold comes from.

Marvel at the Mayan jade

The Maya are well known for their jade figurines, masks, and jewelry, all created with sharp chisels made of obsidian stone. Jade's green color is of special significance to the Maya because it symbolizes sprouting, green maize. Jade ear plugs (earrings) are in great demand right now, but time travelers should not try and wear them. The Maya start making holes for their ear plugs from infancy, which is how they get them to fit.

Top Tip

Better to barter

Time travelers should remember to bring something to barter, as there is no money in Chichén Itzá. If you take some cacao beans with you, you will be able to exchange them for anything you want.

WHAT TO WEAR

Time travelers will find it easy to spot a person's status at Chichén Itzá. The ruling nobles wear expensive clothes that dazzle and amaze with their splendor. Workers and peasants stick to plain, practical clothes.

Dress like a noble

Dressing like the Chichén Itzá nobles may not be possible for time travelers. Only the rulers, nobles, and priests at the top of society wear elaborate headdresses, jade, bone, and shell jewelry, leather sandals, clothes with intricate patterns, and capes made from the skins of wild animals. They tattoo their bodies and file down their front teeth into points. Time travelers wishing to look like a noble should be aware that there is a waiting list for jaguar-skin capes this year.

Top Tip

Stare at the flat heads

Normally it is rude to stare, but if you see a noble with a flat-shaped head you will be expected to admire its beauty. The shape is achieved by tying a board to an infant's head to flatten it over time. This is considered the height of beauty in Chichén Itzá.

Dress like a peasant

Instead of dressing like a noble, many time travelers prefer to dress like a worker or peasant, so they can blend into the crowd. Ordinary Chichén Itzá males wear a simple cotton loin cloth around their waists, and females wear a plain square dress called a huipil. Both sexes go barefoot and wear a cape made of cotton or animal skin to cover their shoulders.

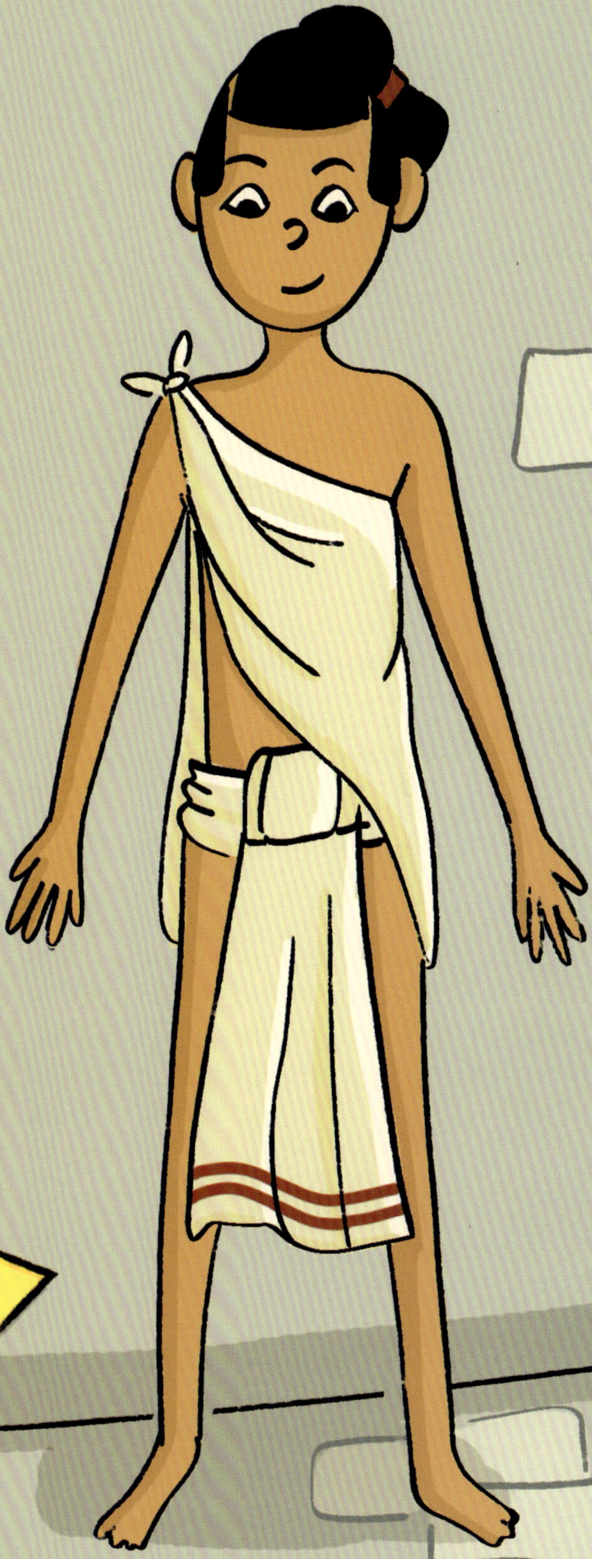

A DAY AT THE BALL GAME

Chichén Itzá is famous for its enormous ball court – the largest ever constructed in a Mayan city. No stay at the city would be complete without watching a ball game. However, time travelers need to be prepared. Mayan ball games are deadly affairs where people can be sacrificed as part of the proceedings.

What are the rules?

To play the Mayan ball game, two teams compete to score goals by firing a heavy, rubber ball through rings positioned along the court's sides. Players can use all parts of their body, except their hands and feet. In Chichén Itzá, the game is slightly different from other cities because a bat can be used to hit the ball. To protect themselves, players wear thick padding around their waists, knees, and elbows. Make sure to watch out for a stray ball – it will hurt if it accidently lands in the crowd!

Top Tip

Leave early to avoid the death

The ball game is designed to represent its mythological origins and humans are sometimes sacrificed to symbolize the killing of the brothers and the underworld gods. Time travelers don't have to stay for this part of the game!

The ball court rings are about 26 feet (8 m) off the ground.

This ball-court wall carving (right) shows the game's mythological origins and the statue (below) shows one of the ancient ball players.

The story of the game

Time travelers can see the ball game's mythological origins carved on the ball court's outer walls. According to the story, two brothers Jun Junajpu and Wuqub' Junajpu awoke the gods of the underworld by playing the ball game too loudly. The gods challenged the brothers to a match, but once in the underworld they were deceived and beheaded. However, the brothers were avenged by their children, the Hero Twins, who eventually defeated the underworld gods.

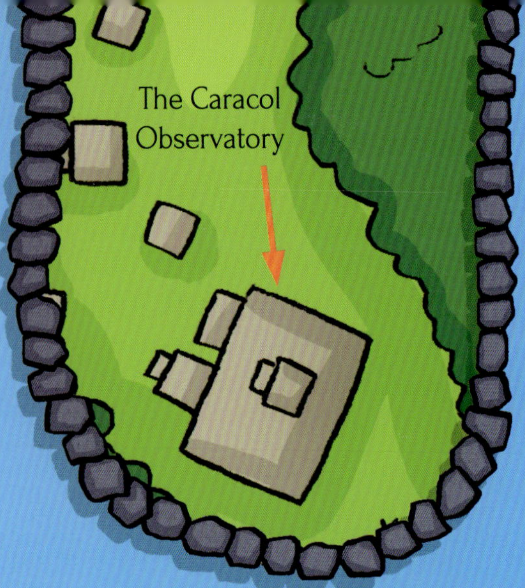

SEE THE STARS

To enjoy a favorite Chichén Itzá night out, time travelers can visit the Caracol Observatory. From the windowed dome of this raised building, you can watch the priests study the skies and track the movements of the stars and planets. This is how the Maya calculate the passing of time and make predictions about the future.

Predict the future

The Caracol Observatory has been specially built to observe celestial objects moving across the sky. These movements, which include the sun, moon, and planets such as Venus, are then used to plan important events. These events may be the crowning of a new ruler, the decision to go to war or the need for blood-letting rituals or human sacrifices. The priests also believe the skies can help predict the future, such as the coming of the end of the world. What predictions will you make from the Caracol Observatory?

What day is it?

In Chichén Itzá people calculate the time based on the passing of day and night. Day turning to night represents one main cycle of everyday Mayan life. The Maya record these cycles in detailed calendars. One of these calendars has 365 days in a year. Another calendar, called the Long Count, gives the starting date for the creation of the world as August 11, 3114 BCE.

Top Tip

Use your fingers and toes

The Maya count in groups of 20 and use all of their fingers and toes to do so. Time travelers should therefore get ready to take off their shoes and socks when discussing numbers.

COMMUNICATE LIKE A MAYAN

In Chichén Itzá, communication is key. The ruler makes decisions based on information from the priests, and orders are sent out to the people along the city's road networks. Chichén Itzá's spoken language may be hard for time travelers to understand, unless you come from Central America. In the 21st century, dozens of Mayan languages are still spoken there.

Be a scribe for the day

Scribes help the ruler govern the people. They are often born into the job and serve as close advisers to the ruler. However, as a special offer to time travelers, the Chichén Itzá scribes have agreed to give them a day's work experience. This will include teaching visitors how to write their names in glyphs, the Mayan form of writing.

Top Tip

Learn the language

The dozens of Mayan languages are all based on one mother language called proto-Mayan. First spoken in around 2200 BCE, proto-Mayan later evolved into languages such as Ch'olan and Tzeltalan. The people of Chichén Itzá speak a language called Itzá, which is where they get their name. Time travelers should try to use some common Itzá words such as Ja (water), Jun (one), and Il (see).

Uncode the glyphs

Mayan writing is made up of picture words, called glyphs, that are arranged in blocks. Many of these glyphs are inscribed onto walls, pieces of wood, and tall stelae columns. Other glyphs are written in books made of folded bark paper, called codices. Codices open like a fan and contain details of prophesies, astronomical events, calendars, and stories from Mayan mythology. The Maya love asking time travelers to uncode their glyphs. What do you think they say?

VISIT QUICK!

The residents of Chichén Itzá believe they live in the greatest city of the Mayan civilization. However, even they admit it cannot last forever. Priests watching the stars are predicting a time of great turbulence and terror. So visit now, before Chichén Itzá's golden age comes to a close.

Chichén Itzá's decline

Chichén Itzá was one of the last great cities of the Mayan civilization. After dominating for over 200 years, the city declined as the rulers' power diminished. Some believe a series of droughts stopped people from believing in their rulers' ability to understand the gods' wishes. By around 1250 CE, the city of Mayapan took over as the leading regional power, although some people still lived on in Chichén Itzá. By the 15th century, many Maya had returned to living in villages.

The end of the Maya

Between 1527 and 1546 the Yucatan peninsula was conquered by the Spanish and Chichén Itzá was turned into a cattle farm. The Spanish went on to conquer all of Mesoamerica and treated the Maya badly wherever they went. The Maya were often enslaved, executed for being heathens, or killed by diseases introduced from Europe. Over time, those Maya left alive often adopted the culture and religion of the Spanish. But despite this, many native Mayan customs and languages survived into the 21st century.

Top Tip

Drop in on the discovery

Time travelers with archaeology in mind may want to drop in during the 19th century. At that time, Chichén Itzá was rediscovered after being reclaimed by the jungle. Many other Mayan cities were also discovered during the 19th century, leading modern people to wonder about those who once lived there.

GLOSSARY

Cenote A deep, underground pool of water found in Central America.

Ceremony An event which celebrates something, such as an achievement, anniversary, or religious occasion.

City-state A state that has its own government and consists of a city and the area around it.

Culture A pattern of behavior that is shared by a society or group of people.

Delicacy A type of food that is rare or expensive.

Equinox An equinox occurs when the position of the sun is exactly over the equator.

Export Goods or services taken from one country or region to another for purposes of trade.

Glyph A symbol or picture that represents a word in some ancient languages, such as Mayan.

Heathen A person that does not believe in god or belong to a common religion.

Jade A green mineral used for jewelry and carvings.

Mesoamerica The region of Mexico and Central America once occupied by the Maya and Aztecs.

Myth A traditional story made up to explain certain events in history or nature.

Obsidian A dark, hard, glasslike volcanic rock.

Prophecy A prediction or knowledge of the future.

Quetzal A bird with brightly colored feathers which lives in the jungles of South America.

Ritual A ceremony or action performed in a customary way.

Stela An upright stone column or slab inscribed with words or pictures.

Stingray spine A sharp spine at the end of a ray's tail that can cause injury and even kill.

Tapir A hoofed, pig-like mammal with a long snout.

FURTHER INFORMATION

Books

Maya Myths and Legends, Janie Havemeyer, Jump!, Inc., 2025.

The Ancient Maya Times. Nick Hunter, Oxford University Press, 2024.

The Rise and Fall of the Maya Civilization. D. R. Faust, Bearport Publishing, 2025.

Websites

A website for kids focusing on the Mayan ball game: **https://www.chichenitza.com/mayan-ball-game**

A Smithsonian website about the Maya, their beliefs and their calenders: **maya.nmai.si.edu**

INDEX